D0787680

United States Regions

Great Plains Region

Anastasia Suen

rourkeeducationalmedia.com

Scan for Related Titles
and Teacher Resources

Before Reading:

Building Academic Vocabulary and Background Knowledge

Before reading a book, it is important to tap into what your child or students already know about the topic. This will help them develop their vocabulary, increase their reading comprehension, and make connections across the curriculum.

1. Look at the cover of the book. What will this book be about?
2. What do you already know about the topic?
3. Let's study the Table of Contents. What will you learn about in the book's chapters?
4. What would you like to learn about this topic? Do you think you might learn about it from this book? Why or why not?
5. Use a reading journal to write about your knowledge of this topic. Record what you already know about the topic and what you hope to learn about the topic.
6. Read the book.
7. In your reading journal, record what you learned about the topic and your response to the book.
8. After reading the book complete the activities below.

Content Area Vocabulary
Read the list. What do these words mean?

aquifer
bison
claim
economy
elevation
glaciers
hemisphere
prospector
potholes
waterfowl

After Reading:

Comprehension and Extension Activity

After reading the book, work on the following questions with your child or students in order to check their level of reading comprehension and content mastery.

1. What are some reasons as to why many people do not live in the Great Plains region? (Summarize)
2. How did glaciers affect the land known as the Great Plains? (Asking questions)
3. Why did Congress pass the Indian Removal Act? (Infer)
4. How did settlers affect the lives of the Native Americans living in the Great Plains? (Infer)
5. Explain what an aquifer is. (Summarize)

Extension Activity

What is an aquifer? How does it work? An aquifer is a layer of water found underground. The water comes from rain and river or lake overflow and seeps into the ground. To better understand how this works you will need roughly 1 cup (250 ml) of various ground samples such as dirt, gravel, sand, and clay. Use a disposable plastic cup for each material and poke a hole in the bottom of each cup to allow water to flow out. Now, pour water into the cups one at a time. You will need to hold the cup over a large bowl, sink, or the ground since water will come out of the holes. Prior to pouring the water, guess which ground sample will hold the water? Which sample will let the water flow freely through? What samples will make the best aquifer to hold the water underground?

Table of Contents

The Great Plains Region

The Great Plains are in the middle of our country. This region is made up of dry grassland. It falls between the Midwest region's farmland to the east and the Mountain region to the west. The Great Plains states include Montana, North Dakota, South Dakota, Wyoming, Colorado, Nebraska, Kansas, New Mexico, Oklahoma, and Texas.

Though few people live in the Great Plains, the land supports plant and animal life. A wide variety of grasses grow. Animals in the region include lizards, prairie dogs, weasels, and rattlesnakes.

The Great Plains has a variety of grasses, including blue grama, buffalo grass, crested wheatgrass, and little bluestem.

The weather in the Great Plains is one of extremes. Most of the land in the Great Plains is flat. There are very few trees, so there is nothing to slow down the wind. Cold winds blow down from the Arctic, bringing cold, dry weather. Warm winds blow in from the Gulf of Mexico, bringing warm, wet weather. Warm, dry air blows across the land, too. These winds come from the deserts in the southwest.

The low lying prairie, gets a lot of rain. The grasses there grow 6 feet (2 meters) tall. The high plains border more closely with the Rocky Mountains. They get very little rain, and so the grass is shorter. The vast grasslands are a great place for ranchers to graze their cattle. The Great Plains is also a good place for growing wheat, corn, and sunflowers.

When dry weather hits wet weather it can start a storm. The warm air spins up, and a tornado is formed. The winds can reach 300 miles per hour (482 kilometers per hour)!

Many tornadoes form in the Great Plains. The area where they form is called Tornado Alley.

Forming the Plains

Long ago, there were **glaciers** across the land. The giant sheets of ice were very heavy. The glaciers changed the land as they slowly slid by.

Glaciers made holes in the land, which filled up with rain and snow. These prairie **potholes** make a great place for **waterfowl** to swim.

Prairie potholes are wetlands. They are home to more than half of the waterfowl in North America.

Rocks and gravel along the Missouri River show evidence of glaciers long ago.

As the glaciers moved, they made the land flat. They pushed away the rocks and gravel and formed lakes as the ice melted. Deposits of rocks and sediments along riverbanks show that glaciers played a big role in shaping the land in the Great Plains.

Plains Indians hunted on horseback, using spears, bows and arrows, or clubs to take down the buffalo.

People have been living on the plains for more than ten thousand years. When glaciers covered waters in the north, tribes from Asia crossed into North America. The Native Americans who lived in the Great Plains hunted buffalo, or **bison**. Buffalo were essential to their way of life. The plains tribes used different parts of the buffalo to make food, clothes, knives, tools, and decorations.

Bison on the Plains

Long ago, bison lived on the plains. A bison can grow very large. Some can weigh more than one ton. That's 2,000 pounds (907 kilograms)! Herds of bison ate the grass on the plains, and the people who lived there hunted them for meat. They used bison hides for clothing and shelter.

Bison are very heavy. But they are also very fast. A bison can run 40 miles per hour (64 kilometers per hour)!

Black Hills

You can see where the glacier stopped moving across the plains in the Black Hills of South Dakota and Wyoming. The land here is not flat. There is a thick evergreen forest in the hills. The native Lakota gave the hills their name because there were so many trees growing there that the hills looked black.

You can visit the Black Hills National Forest. The Black Hills are 125 miles (201 kilometers) long and 65 miles (104 kilometers) wide.

General George Custer
1839–1876

The Sioux War

In 1874, General George Custer came to the Black Hills. Custer sent news that there was gold in the Black Hills. Thousands of people came to look for the gold, but the land belonged to the Sioux people. A war between the U.S. and the Sioux ended when U.S. troops forced the Sioux to surrender and moved the tribes to reservations.

Sitting Bull was chief of the Sioux people. He led his people in the Sioux War. They defeated Custer and his men at the Battle of Little Big Horn.

Sitting Bull
Birth unknown – 1890

13

When gold was discovered in the Black Hills, many settlers moved to the area. The Black Hills were mined for gold, silver, coal, and other minerals. Their forests were harvested for timber. Today, the **economy** of the Black Hills relies more on tourism. People enjoy camping, horseback riding, rock climbing, snowmobiling, and taking in the area's natural beauty.

One part of the Black Hills is very famous. The heads of four presidents are carved in the rock. Each year, 3 million people visit Mount Rushmore.

Gutzon Borglum was the sculptor who created Mount Rushmore. He made many models for his workmen to use as guides. They worked from 1927 to 1941.

From left to right are George Washington, Thomas Jefferson, Theodore Roosevelt, and Abraham Lincoln.

The High Plains

The high plains stretch across the middle of the country. They begin in Montana and end in Texas.

The weather is cold and windy, and the area receives little rainfall. Despite the lack of rain, agriculture is an important part of the high plains economy. Water is drawn from a large **aquifer** under the land's surface.

Bordering the Rocky Mountains, the **elevation** of the high plains is 4,500 to 6,500 feet (1,370 to 1,980 meters).

In Nebraska, there is sand above the aquifer. The Nebraska Sandhills cover almost 20,000 square miles (64,750 square kilometers). It is the largest area of sand dunes in the Western **hemisphere**. Deer, coyotes, wild turkeys, badgers, and skunks live here.

Grass keeps the sand in place. Much of the Nebraska Sandhills are protected as a wildlife refuge.

The Spanish first explored the Great Plains when Francisco Vasquez de Coronado led an expedition there. In 1541, he led more than 1,000 men from Mexico to Kansas in search of a city of gold.

Coronado and his men went north to Quivira. Today that land is in the state of Kansas.

Because he did not find the gold cities that legends spoke of, Coronado's expedition was a failure.

Francisco Vasquez
de Coronado
1510–1554

In 1801, Spain sold part of its North American **claim** to France. Three years later, France sold the land to the United States in the Louisiana Purchase. It doubled the size of the United States. But much of the land was unexplored. President Thomas Jefferson sent Lewis and Clark to explore and map the land.

Louisiana Purchase

The route Lewis and Clark took from the Atlantic to the Pacific Ocean in their exploration of North America.

Sacagawea was living in a Mandan village in North Dakota when Lewis and Clark came. She traveled with them and guided them across the country.

Sacagawea
1788 – Death unknown

After the Louisiana Purchase, Native tribes were moved to lands in Kansas, Nebraska, Iowa, and Oklahoma.

Settlers in the American South wanted more land. Native Americans had a large area of hunting ground that settlers could not use. In 1830, Congress passed the Indian Removal Act. Tribes across the south were moved to the land bought in the Louisiana Purchase.

Apache Fry Bread

Ingredients:

1 cup water

2 1/2 cups flour

1 teaspoon baking powder

1 teaspoon salt

Directions:

Mix flour, baking powder, and salt in a bowl. Add water and stir to make dough. Place dough on a floured surface. Roll with rolling pin until dough is 1/2 inch thick. Cut into squares. Fry in 2 inches of hot oil. Turn until brown on both sides.

In 1892, President Lincoln signed a new law. It was called the Homestead Act. Now people could claim the land on the plains. They could file a claim for 160 acres (65 hectares) of land. After their claims were filed, these families moved to the plains. They had to live and work on the land for five years. Then they could file for the deed to own the land.

For many years, settlers crossed the plains on their way to settle on the West Coast. Their wagon trains followed the Oregon Trail.

Plains settlers found the land good for farming and ranching. Soon **prospectors** discovered oil, coal, and natural gas. More jobs drew more people to settle in the Great Plains.

For safety, people traveled west in large groups called wagon trains.

Still, few people live in the Great Plains when compared to other parts of the country. Most of the Great Plains is made up of rural areas. The people live in small towns, on farms, and on ranches. Without many nearby cities, many Great Plains people are independent and hard working. The Great Plains is a unique region of the United States and is part of what makes our country great.

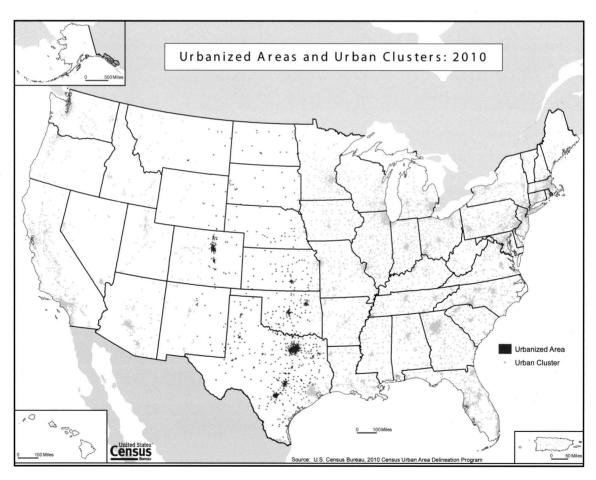

Many people live in urban areas (purple) and urban clusters (green). Few people live in rural (white) areas.

Some areas of the plains are growing. Oil was discovered in Williston, North Dakota. This small farming town became a booming oil town.

State Facts Sheet

Montana

Motto: Gold and Silver.

Nickname: The Treasure State

Capital: Helena

Known for: Wildlife, Glacier Park, Yellowstone Park

Fun Fact: An average square mile in Montana has 1.4 elk, 1.4 pronghorn antelope, and 3.3 deer.

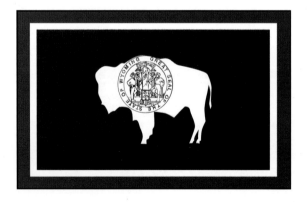

Wyoming

Motto: Equal Rights.

Nickname: The Equality or Cowboy State

Capital: Cheyenne

Known for: Yellowstone Park, Old Faithful Geyser, Jackson Hole, Buffalo Bill, Coal

Fun Fact: Wyoming was the first state to give women the right to vote.

North Dakota

Motto: Liberty and Union, Now and Forever, One and Inseparable.

Nickname: Peace Garden State

Capital: Bismarck

Known for: Badlands, Bison, Rodeos, Wildlife, Sunflowers

Fun Fact: North Dakota has the highest number of millionaires per capita than any other state.

South Dakota

Motto: Under God the People Rule.

Nickname: Mount Rushmore State

Capital: Pierre

Known for: Mount Rushmore, Black Hills Gold, Fossils

Fun Fact: The Homestake Mine is the oldest and largest gold mine in the United States. It produces 15 percent of the nation's gold.

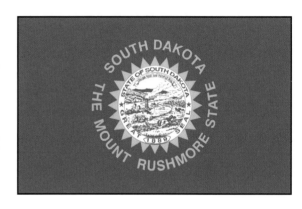

Nebraska

Motto: Equality Before the Law.

Nickname: Cornhusker State

Capital: Lincoln

Known for: Chimney Rock, Fossil Beds

Fun Fact: The largest mammoth fossils ever discovered were found in Lincoln County.

Colorado

Motto: Nothing Without the Deity.
Nickname: The Centennial State
Capital: Denver
Known for: Skiing, Rocky Mountains, Pike's Peak, Forests, Mining
Fun Fact: The world's largest flattop mountain is in Grand Mesa.

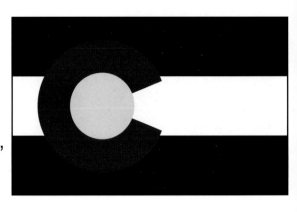

Kansas

Motto: Ad Astra per Aspera (To the Stars Through Difficulties.)
Nickname: Sunflower State
Capital: Topeka
Known for: Dodge City, Cattle, Wheat
Fun Fact: Kansas was the first state to ratify the fifteenth amendment, giving African American men the right to vote.

New Mexico

Motto: It Grows as it Goes.
Nickname: The Land of Enchantment
Capital: Santa Fe
Known for: Beautiful Scenery, Unique Cuisine, Uranium, Roswell
Fun Fact: The state's longest river, the Rio Grande, runs the entire length of New Mexico.

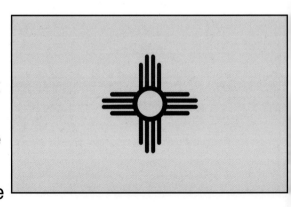

Oklahoma

Motto: Labor Omnia Vincit
  (Labor Conquers all Things.)
Nickname: Sooner State
Capital: Oklahoma City
Known for: Cowboys, Rodeos,
  Former Indian Territory, Oil
Fun Fact: Oklahoma's state capitol
  building is the only capitol in the
  world with an oil well under it.

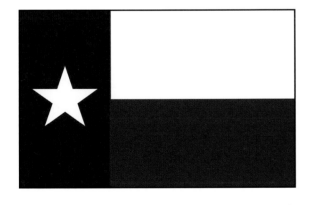

Texas

Motto: Friendship.
Nickname: The Lone Star State
Capital: Austin
Known for: Longhorn Cattle, The
  Alamo, Cowboys, Oil, Barbecue
Fun Fact: Texas was an independent
  nation from 1836 to 1845.

Glossary

aquifer (AK-wuh-fer): a layer of rock or sand that can hold water

bison (BAHY-suhn): a large animal with a big shaggy head, humped back, and short horns

claim (klaym): a demand or request for something considered one's due

economy (i-KAH-nuh-mee): system of buying, selling, and making things in a place

elevation (el-uh-VAY-shuhn): the land's height above sea level

glaciers (GLAY-shurz): giant sheets of ice

hemisphere (HEM-uhss-fihr): one half of a sphere, especially of the Earth

potholes (POT-hohlz): holes in the surface of the ground or a road

prospectors (PRAHS-spektors): people who search for gold, oil, coal, or other natural resources

waterfowl (WAW-tur-foul): birds that live in the water

Index

Show What You Know

1. Why is the weather in the Great Plains so extreme?
2. Why did explorers come to the Great Plains?
3. Where can you find water in the prairie?
4. Why were tribes moved to the Great Plains?
5. Why do so few people live in the Great Plains region?

Websites to Visit

www.nps.gov/badl

www.nps.gov/tapr

www.nps.gov/trte

Author

Anastasia Suen's family has lived in the northern plains for more than 200 years. They farmed the land for many generations. Today she lives with her family in Plano, Texas.

Meet The Author!
www.meetREMauthors.com

www.rourkeeducationalmedia.com

PHOTO CREDITS: Cover © bgsmith, Brandon Seidel, Kubrak78, knapjames, jovannig; Title page © konglinguang; page 3 © Robert Ford; page 5 © John De Bord; page 7 © PeteDraper; page 8 © Erickson Photography, panbazil; page 9 © kavram; page 10 © Smithsonian American Art Museum; page 11 © Julie Lubick; page 12 © Steve Geer; page 13 © MarinaGold, Willierossin; page 14 © coburn77; page 15 © Galyna Andrushko; page 16 © Brendan Hunter; page 17 © threespeedjones; page 18 © Library of Congress, Wikipedia; page 19 © spirit of america; page 20 © Sky Light Pictures; page 21 © Lokibaho, takayuki; page 22 © ZU_09; page 23 © Theo. R. Davis; page 25 © Zorandim

Edited by: Jill Sherman

Cover design by: Jen Thomas
Interior design by: Rhea Magaro

Library of Congress PCN Data

Great Plains Region / Anastasia Suen
(United States Regions)
ISBN 978-1-62717-670-5 (hard cover)
ISBN 978-1-62717-792-4 (soft cover)
ISBN 978-1-62717-909-6 (e-Book)
Library of Congress Control Number: 2014934378

Printed in the United States of America, North Mankato, Minnesota

Also Available as: